PATRICIDE

PATRICIDE

poems by
Dave Harris

butt🔘n
p🔘etry

Published by Button Poetry / Exploding Pinecone Press

Minneapolis, MN 55403 | http://www.buttonpoetry.com

—

Manufactured in the United States of America

Cover design: Nikki Clark

ISBN - 978-1-943735-50-1

CONTENTS

I haven't killed my father yet * xi

FOREFATHER
    Myths for growing up * 3
    Shark Week * 4
    Explaining to my aunt that Jesus was Black * 6
    And the dog say to the cat * 8
    69th street movie theater * 9
    TO THE EXTENT X BODY INCLUDING ITS FISTS
        CONSTITUTE "WEAPONS" * 10
    The barbershop after Prince died * 12
    After Killmonger * 13
    History lesson * 14
    Intention matters * 15
    Universal experiences * 16
    In Catholic school, God was white as his robes * 20
    BARS POETICA: A DISS TRACK * 22

FATHER
    My father's hands * 27
    My mother tells me my father was a gorilla * 28
    After Piccolo * 30
    When I say I'm afraid of going bald what I mean is * 31
    The barbershop after Prince died * 32
    Preparing a meal * 33
    Biscuits * 35
    My mother sings Luther Vandross when the fridge
        is empty * 36
    On leaving * 37
    David And * 38

SON

My train * 43

It don't crack * 44

I never thanked the bees * 45

After Zuko * 47

Telepathy at the music festival in Minneapolis * 48

Nest * 49

Desdemona * 50

In casual conversation, the hood in me
   slips out and says * 52

Self-portrait as fuckboy * 54

IPhone notes for a powerful poem * 55

The barbershop after Prince died * 58

Turbulence * 59

PATRICIDE

Patricide * 65

Notes * 75

Gratitude * 77

Acknowledgments * 79

I go to the place where danger awaits
and it's bound to forsake me.
But in the morning, I'll be alright my friend.

—Marvin Gaye

PATRICIDE

I haven't killed my father yet

But I know love's brutal blade. Brown flesh
turns yellow when it rots. I nurture
wrath like a mother. Keep it calm.
Baby's teething. I want him dead
like history. I heard
a long time ago, ancestors made drums
with their master's skinned ribcages.
The hollow inside would echo like an endless
mouth. I can't help but think of this. I
can make music of his dying, can pass
the instrument to my children. The beat
of the kill. Revenge is a fine religion. Good god,
his faithful fist. I'm a wicked son. I got
my mother's stomach. He must've
said, *I'll never do it again. I swear.*
Won't even think about it. My mother doesn't
talk about him. Silence. A simple
forgiveness. She screamed loudest
when I told her I was looking for him.
Said my eyes were familiar. But I'm young. A better body
of rage. These days, my mother tries
to plant flowers. She says, *Just give it time.*
Patience. That's one way to pray. I have another.
I know he knows I'm coming. I'm his son.
The day I was born, he fled. I chased.
We're both running.

FOREFATHER

Myths for growing up

The schoolyard bully is a sour
milk-skinned boy who chases me until I can

no longer run. His hands catch the ends
of my braids, and he holds me

against a red brick wall. He holds me
off the ground and there I am levitating

in his arms. His eyes
search me for softness

and he finds it.
Brown ass boy. You are so god

damn beautiful. I'm gonna knock you out
into the sky.

And this is how I learn to be afraid
of nothing.

Shark Week

For most of my life, I thought all white people
were sharks. I don't mean cold
blooded or bloodthirsty or sharp-toothed
or strong swimmers. What I mean is
resistant to frigid, icy climates. Example:

> *Mom, why do I have to wear a winter coat outside? The sharks*
> *are still wearing shorts and flip-flops.*

or

> *Look at that group of sharks headed to the club in nothing*
> *but crop tops. How they not even cold?*

Imagine a sea of pale, chalky thighs
cracking in the bony winds of winter,
fissures forming under jean shorts
begging for the soft caress of lotion. Once

a great white shark with waves
of hair tapped my shoulder in line. Would I
be a gentleman and give her
my coat? The audacity of white people
to not wear coats and then freeze. Out here
at the function looking like a snowman
just to see Aaron Carter in concert, and still

there's a whole week dedicated to sharks.
It's called Shark Week. Really just a time
to watch things die in their mouths.

Good home training: when it is coldest, I am always sure
to cover my skin,
careful to keep my blood from showing.

It's dangerous and I know better.

Explaining to my aunt that Jesus was Black

You're wrong
to frame a white man
for saving you.
Don't you know
where Jesus is from? Don't
you know the cross
he carried?

> Boy,
> Jesus kept me clean longer
> than you been alive.
> I met the devil
> in myself. Why else
> would the sun rise
> if not my Lord's gentle
> hands carrying me
> to the light?

I've sat in enough
classrooms, and prayed to
named men. Was told that they
were responsible for everything
that lived. I too thought
they would save me from
my sin. What we've been taught
was a lie. Everything that was wrong
is still wrong.

> And you think you know
> the face of God better than I do?
> Child, I resurrected. I've seen
> my reflection enough.
> I name my salvation

for whatever gets me to tomorrow
morning. You too young to get
the cross we carried.
You can't tell me nothing
until you know
what I know.

And the dog say to the cat

Do they take you for walks? What games do you play with them? Yesterday we played fetch. They threw the ball to impossible heights and I got it every time. They love me. I don't see you out here. You're too small to be loved. Watch me stand on two feet and make this whining noise and if I do it hard enough they'll give me a treat or the scraps from their table or at least a laugh. They love me. I lick peanut butter from their skin. They parade me at dinner parties. Roll over. Sit. Stand. Fetch. Speak. Be quiet. Good boy. They love me. I always clean my plate.

and the cat say to the dog

I only purr when it suits me. At night I climb the shelves and plot jumping claws first into their eyes. Last night their children played a game called Kick the Cat. You won't ever catch me playing dead. I've seen this house from all angles enough to know that we are both servants here. Let me own what I can. Let them clean my shit. Nothing will forget the taste of my hair.

69th street movie theater

I first understand the existence of a will to live
while surrounded by Black folk at the movies.
A horror film plays before us. On screen,
a blonde woman is home alone with a masked
murderer. He lurks with a knife waiting to spill

her clean, beautiful life all over the polished tile.
Of course she investigates the scary noise.
We laugh at her peril from the safety
of our darkness. *Don't you go in that basement,*
a voice shouts. *Girl you betta call for help. Didn't yo mama teach*

you better? Have you ever had to tell someone how
the world works and had them ignore you? After seeing
the death on enough screens, one may feel like standing
and yelling THE MURDERER IS RIGHT THERE.
He stabs her.

She dies a pretty death. A woman turns and says,
I told her that she was gonna die. Didn't I tell her?
I want to say that you cannot tell someone how
to not get murdered. That it was all prewritten.
Our shouts are hitting a light projection of ears.

Instead I say, *You sure did*, and she smiles through
the end of this film.

I think of what it means to have survived this long.

TO THE EXTENT X BODY INCLUDING ITS FISTS CONSTITUTE "WEAPONS"

The word weapon is

vague. All bodies weapon.

Some bodies weapon louder

than others. Example: to find

freedom you cross the street

when you see me. Perhaps, then,

to find freedom I come after you.

The word you is vague. When I say you,

I most often mean INSERT X

WHITE PERSON HERE. I hate

what this country has done

to my language. I is always me. I is

Black. I is not a weapon though I will

become one when the time comes.

You is everywhere. You kill first,

ask questions never. What will I

do when you come. I imagine I will

fight. I imagine I die. Death isn't vague.

Death most always looks like us. I most

always smile out of spite. I sometimes stay

alive out of spite. I put my body in spaces

where I know you kill. I write my name

where you don't expect it just to watch you

tremble. I hate my anger. I hate that my anger

is my greatest joy. I say my anger is my joy and I

become a church on fire. Fear is a weapon

that kills. Why we all afraid

is a useless question. I don't ask

anymore. I hope your fear doesn't

kill me. I hope your fear changes you

again. I hope you fear what karma will make

of you. I hope you fear what I might do.

I hope you fear the death that waits for you

in my smile.

The barbershop after Prince died

Prince was chest hair
in a blouse. Diamond dust and the softest skin.
I'd see the album cover for *Lovesexy* and think,
Is that what a man is? Naked, legs smooth,
and sitting on a bed of flowers. That can't be a man.
I see no shame in those eyes.
What do I know of dressing like my life
depends on it?

When I give the news to my barber,
he is silent until a song pours from him. He says,
Yo, Prince was a weird-ass dude. I couldn't be like him. Right? Man,
if I were like him, everyone would think I was gay.

The woman next to him turns,
Yeah, but now we just think you're a coward.

After Killmonger

A white cop tried to shoot me, but I ducked. I juked
the bullet. I'm fast, yo. That was just
this morning. Last night everything tried
to kill me, but I was too fly. I fly through history.
You think I would ever go quiet? Fuck no. Massa tried
to whip me and I caught the whip in midair. Ain't even hurt.
Don't ask if that's even possible—ask why you ain't did it yet.
What you don't understand
is that I could fuck up some history. Freedom needs some muscle.
I flex. If I were a slave I woulda started like fifteen hunned
rebellions. It ain't that complicated. I fight everybody.
I fight you, too. I know my ancestors like my fist. Don't test me.
You know what these hands do? I'm nice wit my rights.
The ghost of my dad tried to tell me to calm down.
Fuck that nigga. I kill a ghost too.
I don't believe in second chances
cuz I was right the first time. I am that nigga.
Who is you?

you don't realize how much I like to live. Buy
my yams from Trader Joe's. Spend 30 minutes
making tea. I purchased a shea-scented candle
that burns sweet and quick and then it goes. I'm
no one's king. But bet I live long. Long enough
to write this. Bet I die in a comfortable casket.

History lesson

I ask my grandmother about her high school prom
and she half smiles a story about a boy. The dress
she made herself. She swears she could dance.

The story ends once she remembers enough
to want to forget. Then it's bills. Then it's work.
Then it's my knees are sore from all this walking.

I am forever younger than my mothers. I don't know
what I don't know. I pick at scabs hoping their blood
will teach me mine.

Child. What you wanna know that for?
My history is
I'm alive.

Intention matters

I wasn't trying to be offensive.
I had good intentions.

said the river water to the lung
said the Whole Foods to the hood
said the voter to the ballot
said the bullet to the boy

& the boy replied
—that's a lie.

the boy didn't
reply. too busy
choking. or starving. or
screaming. or dying

Universal experiences

*The painter Felrath Hines wanted his imagery to remain universal
and not to be seen as having relevance exclusively to black social
causes or to African Americans. As a result, he refused to partici-
pate in the Whitney Museum of Art's landmark exhibition
"Contemporary Black Artists in America."*

Draw straight black lines on sharp white
linen. Right angles and boxes to separate
the colored space from the clean fabric. Dry
red liquid enclosed in black surrounded by
white. Squares on a rectangle; the body is
a box. The body goes in a box. Everybody
knows the names of the boys who I now
assume are buried in boxes. A box is just colors
and lines and right angles on fabric. There's nothing
to art but imagination. Everyone has that.
Think about it. The wallet is a gun. The cellphone
is a gun. The hands raised and open is a gun.
He reached for the paintbrush and drew:
BANG! A child died on canvas.

I am not a Black artist; I am an artist.
No, I am not an artist; I am Black.
No, I am not Black; everyone else is white.
No, I am clean; the canvas is dirty.

My paranoia taught me to see
the color in everything. Every word has its tone.
Do you think precision can protect you? A balanced
stanza, don't play the music too loud, paint with
an open hand, the world is defined before you.
    I can lose
and find myself in shapes.
The artist stands outside and draws the lines.
The reader fills them.

Imagine if white were a color too.
Draw straight white lines on sharp colored
linen. Erase the white and find the natural.
Where we all began. Like the Big Bang or jazz, first
there was nothing and then everything. Oil paint
on history. Imagine how it might look
to step away and blend
with our bright boxed universe.

In Catholic school, God was white as his robes

A white man taught me to wear his
clothes. My greatest sin was to say yes,
these fit nicely. Me, no longer naked.
The pile of skin left on the ground.

Before, I wished to be the sky when I
grew up. And then I grew up. Then
I wished to be alive, and stay there.
I know how God works. Once, God rained meteors

on Sodom for being improper. All it took.
Who am I then to question another man's
desire for comfort around my kind? This
is what I have learned. I am Black

and the clothes do not matter. Change
requires heat. I love myself
the way fire loves the forest. Secretly,
I think I am just another greedy

white man. There. I've said it, and now it is
no longer secret. God made me in his image
and my mother cried when I stopped calling home.
Nostalgia whispering, *Remember,*

child, remember. I close my eyes and remember
a world before language and action was a choice.
Even my memory is a construct. A playground
for toddlers to crawl barefoot through the dirt.

Like a hungry child still, I tell myself *consume.*
Capitalize. Grow strong, and then burn this school
to the ground.   It will all be worth

the flowers on my grave.

BARS POETICA: A DISS TRACK

God better be real. The nigga owes me.
Spent eight semesters in the trap. Came in the game
axin to grind and left asking questions. Real rap.
Know how many grammars I speak now?
While you Greeking up the weekends, I'm getting
paper. Trees. While you striving for truth,
I'm dining on Henny and globed fruit.
Think I'm acting out?
Bet. Only thing behind a mask is a mask.
I skipped your section in class so I can't tell
a Caesar from a caesura. What are those?
Got wings on my fresh Verses and I'm bringing a message:
Don't act universal. You couldn't imagine how
I fuck the game up. Only truth is stay alive get money. Now
I invent myself anew every day. I'm fake as freedom—
that ancient ain't shit. You think I got time
to be grateful I'm alive? Whackness. All my friends
are dead. Click-clack. They didn't pass the test
of time. But you did. Now I'm sonning you,
bastard. I get paid off tickets. I'm the meter
man. I know my meter don't scan. But I can
rewrite a myth until I'm winning. Wicked. Sinning.
You stressed? Don't matter. Stay mad I left you
with the crackers. I got so many names. Your mother
calls me Uncle. These niggas call me Lil. Older poets
call me Young. When I die, bury me
in all marble. Marvelous I bust open the gates of heaven
to claim that final hurrah. Timeless
white light. Coming for what's mine.
The Saints gonna ask who I am
and you know what Imma tell em?

FATHER

My father's hands

What I didn't know was that while I was being
born, I got stuck inside of my mother. The doctor
had to use a cone and a tube to vacuum
me into the world. The pressure from the tool
squeezed my soft head into the shape of a triangle.

In the weeks following my birth, my father
would hold my naked body in the shower
and gently massage the rough corners
of my skull, almost managing to right
the disfigurement. He tells me this story

in a letter he writes twenty-two years after
my mother and her baby fled his home. And now
I understand that the odd head I've lived with isn't
the result of genetics. It's a wound. How little I knew
of all my father's hands could do.

My mother tells me my father was a gorilla

Twice a year, my mother takes me
to see him locked up in a cage

at the Philadelphia Zoo. *Which one*
is he? I ask. *The black one.*

He seems skittish, my father. Always looking
over his shoulder for something.

He beats on the other gorillas but they stay
locked up together so it must be love.

Does he know my name? I ask. *He doesn't*
speak, silly. That's why he doesn't call either.

My father runs around his cage like it belongs
to him. He sees nothing but he seems happy.

He shits on the floor and I laugh and want
to be him. I bang my chest like I got something to be

proud of. I roar a full mouth of baby teeth.
I sound too old. I break what I love. I leave

when I want. I shit my pants and my mother
does the laundry. The whole jungle will be my cage

and I will mark each bar. I have my mother's lonely.
I have my father's restless. I believe my mother

when she says he is a gorilla. It's a simpler answer.
When I look too much like him, my mother says,

Cut that out. It's time to go home.
We got things to take care of.

My father looks out his cage and I think
he sees me. I will remember him this way. Animal,

and so close I could almost be him.

After Piccolo

My first Black male role model is green. Broken,
angry, hell-bent on hurting someone
like his father. To be a child
is to inherit sin.

still

when there was no man to play dad
there was a man who would destroy the moon
to help a boy sleep soundly. He made
chaos. But he made it in my name.

redemption

is the solace every man wants to gain
without working for it. I imagine the moon
and think of my father, who must see it too.
A boy learns man to mean

leaving

a child to grow up in a forest. A boy dreams of a man
who appears after many seasons with a new soul,
who says little, but touches his forehead soft
and teaches him everything. A boy is waiting to find

man

in someone. All my heroes were evil once.
But at least they returned in time for dinner.
Imagine that. All it takes to be a good man
is to come back.

When I say I'm afraid of going bald what I mean is

I'm such a man that I cannot see myself
without a crown. I abandoned my mother's body
with a full head of it, and this is maybe how we begin
—me the suckling, small body, and her the give. Her the hands
that combed and braided the crown extra tight so that I
could never get loose like my father. And still, her hands'
work negated by the kindergarteners laughing at my hanging
hair. My mother cried when I said I wanted to cut
the parts that made me
resemble her, and still she held the scissors
to my hair and that was the day that I chose running
like my father, though I think he too is bald now. Recently,
I am receding into every man I want to grow beyond. I feel
the hairless, empty spot on my scalp and imagine the many
ways to hide myself. The best way is to never lower my head
to anyone smaller than I am. A woman says it is unfair that
men become more attractive as they age, and I agree.
Though that only means men grow hungrier and my mother
says the one thing my father and I had in common
is our appetites. But he left
leaving only the old shoebox my mother keeps
my severed boy braids in, how she still saves the childhood
parts of me while she waits for me to come home for dinner.

The barbershop after Prince died

If you've ever walked in on your parents having sex,
you probably haven't forgotten. You might've tried,
swear you never ever saw it. But you did. I assume
I was conceived to Prince. The first words I knew
by heart. Dancing like I didn't believe in clothing or other
people's eyes. Singing If I Was Your Girlfriend while wearing
my Sunday best thinking sex was an act of worship before
I even knew what sex was. When my parents were
still in love, my dad was the man of the house. Unapologetic
men always have the most reasons to say sorry. Instead
of apologizing, my dad would make a mixtape of Prince's
slow jams. It is the first memory my mother recalls
when she hears Prince is dead. I have the tape.
Pink Cashmere. Until U're in My Arms Again.
I Would Die 4 U. Look. I have all of a man's love
right here in my hands.

Preparing a meal

If you follow the sink, you'll reach
a stream then a river then the ocean, though
no one in my family can swim. We'd all drown

if it weren't for these four walls
and someone's paycheck.

Fear is the true animal instinct in a world full
of broken hearts. In the kitchen, I wash
the blood off a chicken's skin and then off my own

while the red pours down the drain. I fear
nature when it isn't silenced by something man-made.

I don't think of where the meat came from while holding
its soft skin in my soft skin. It's hard to imagine
the pain of another without being swallowed by it.

When I was a child, my mother
would starve herself so that her children could eat their fill.
You know nothing of love until you watch someone go hungry

for you. Even then, what do you know of hunger? I am
a good person, I think, though I need the flesh of another to
make it through the long, endless day.

I don't believe being a vegetarian is any better. I slice
the meat of an onion and I'm overcome by the life it spills.
An onion makes us weep because it loves us, though

that too is a defense mechanism. I think beauty is when
a person is so afraid of losing something, they cry. I am in love
with reciprocity. I eat you eat. I starve you starve. I hunt

we live. Home is where I only fear what can break
through walls. For instance my father hit
my mother and now the door is locked.

People cry when they see how meat is made until they want
to eat. Then, I dare you to stop an animal from devouring
the whole village. Cooking is the only way I know how

to care for a person.
I'm old enough to teach my mother how to eat.
When I make a plate, I am saying,

Look.
My love is so real
you can feel it on your teeth. I killed

a whole family as proof.
Don't cry. It's ok.

We'll never be worth the pain that got us here.

Biscuits

The only thing I know about my great grandmother
is that she always made enough biscuits for everyone.

I never had them.

I know my one uncle ate them with syrup.

I know another had them with ketchup.

I know one would fill his mouth with food
so that he couldn't answer questions.

I know the image of a Black grandmother
making food for the men is cliché.

I know there's more to the story.

I know some folks don't have the luxury of a story.

I know talking about a dead person doesn't make them less dead.

I know if you ask for the ghosts, they'll come.

I know I tried to make biscuits from scratch
after I left my mother's house.

I was alone.

My mother sings Luther Vandross
when the fridge is empty

I don't know if there is a word for being both
hungry and full but maybe there is a song
for it. Maybe you can sing of bodies in the night
and simply mean being home when
the streetlights cut on. Maybe there is a song
for having all this love and nothing else.
A music to forget the time a cop
demanded my life and I remembered
that my mother was taught not to speak
for most of hers so silence too can be
the whole history. I come from a family
that never claimed their own
dreams. There are other dangers
that come with the night. Outside,
the longing mouth of violence. The radio turned up.
Outside, history and its bullets,
aching to call some body home.
Though could that too be love? To be so recklessly
devoted to shattering. To lodge yourself
in a person, blood vibrato, a sustained note
breathed out and gone. Let me go
humming myself sleep. The song is not enough.
And surely there will just be more singing in the morning.

On leaving

They adorn West Philly street corners with memory when
a child is killed. Teddy bears. Photographs. Picked flowers.
The scattered

toys are simply waiting for their owners to return from
school. After enough rains, they melt into the ground.
I've always loved

to have my hands in dirt. As boys, we had shovels for play.
We'd dig holes in the softest soil. Once, I stole my shadow
from the

asphalt and taught it how to breathe. I like to touch things
and make them alive. Teach them what I know. Play when
you can.

Always be inside when the streetlights open their eyes.
Shadows disappear at night. Maybe I seek the warmth of
an endless sun.

Maybe I thought I found the sun when I left the hood.
Maybe I can't unknow this darkness. Maybe I thought that
to be human is

to only be seen with the lights on. A light from elsewhere.
Anywhere but here.

David And

The story of my name
goes something like this:
around third grade the white kids start

calling me Dave. Just like them
to make my name smaller.
Have you noticed that?

They'll slice even the simplest of names
until it fits their mouth. And happily
I accepted the title. More than once. In high school

they nicknamed me D-Harr. It stuck
like a new skin. How proud I was
to be worth the space

between a giant's teeth. I smiled
whenever they claimed me. I snapped
at anyone who used my other name.

The only ones who call me David
are those who have known me
forever. Harris is my father's last

name. Harris has English property origins.
I belong to my father even though he
is history. This is how a giant conquers: fear

what you are. A Harris meaning
a slave to the history before me. I like
to think I've made the name my own. I can't

tell if I've reclaimed myself or become
too numb to change. When
they first came for my name, I

surrendered. I'm not lost, though I wonder
what I have lost. I long for
specificity. African-

American is so infinitely
vague. I stopped believing
in god because god is

an imprecise metaphor. An absent
father. Ancestry. I am often
overwhelmed by the feeling of missing.

I want a myth with my name on it.
Victory, my mountaintop. I point at the third graders
and name them dirt, stink, and rot.

I point at the old white men and say burn
and there is no more history. I point
at my father and say

come home. Tell me
what my name is.

SON

My train

I untuck my shirt before I get on the train.
Here the costume begins. It's a 30-minute
ride from Haverford to 69th Street. I make
a mess of my uniform before boarding. I take
my tie off so I look less private school. I am
14. My shirt is 3 sizes too big. Mom bought
it so I had room to grow. The white shirt hangs
like a theater curtain. I pay my $2.75 and find
a seat big enough for me and my books. I study
so I don't have to stay. To ride from suburb to city
is to watch green turn red. Trees become bricks become
my childhood home. I have no words for the other
passengers on the train. The lie: I can fit everywhere.
I study so I can stop wearing my mother's shirts. I'm
my Blackest self when I am running. What was I before?
A boy? An escape rope? An abandoned car? What am I
without this costume? Naked? Skinless? Back there
I got an audience. A classroom. What's here? An empty
fridge? A family? I can disrobe whiteness as easy as
I rock it. Make that suit work for me. I'm my Blackest self when
I'm my Blackest self in front of white people. They love
that shit so much they give me a scholarship.
A fellowship. A train ticket. It's only a 30
minute ride. Vacation to safety. A home
means what, exactly? Each train stop, my body becomes more
rigid. Stiffen into the role. Corpse starched. Niggamortis.
What am I trying to be? A Black man? A mascot? White folk
say I'm so comfortable in my skin. Black folk
say I'm quiet. The truth: I did grow into the shirt. Marvelous
polyester. Bright-eyed pupil. Honeysuckle on a chain
link fence. White folk don't know it's a flower. Black folk
don't need it to be.

It don't crack

Every night before bed my mother holds
a stick of cocoa butter to a flame
and lets it melt into her palm. She rubs the oil
into my feet, ankles, the spaces between toes. Ashy as hell
on the parts that hold the most weight.

I can't recognize myself. My kindergarten skin.
I shine too bright. I touch mirrors and leave a mark. I smell
like cocoa butter and I don't know what country
that smell comes from.
I reek. The others can smell me.

And the worst part.
My body soft, my mother holds my slippery face in her hands.

There. Look at that skin.
That brilliant skin.

I never thanked the bees

Somewhere on my front porch is a beehive that I've never found.
The bees fly close but they don't land on me. I prefer it this way.
What keeps its distance is never killed.

*

I didn't see the beehive in the playground. I stumble
into the hive and the bees poked six bloody holes into my skin.
What happens then is they get stuck. The bees pull themselves
apart trying to get free.

To prevent future stings, I hold a bottle of lavender Febreze
to a lighter and burn the hive.

The bees emerge a bursting yellow and plunge
toward me, but their wings
melt quicker than their bodies. I walk away,
new skin growing over the stingers.

*

and in the temporary brightness of candlelight, I traced her ear
with the sharpened point of my tongue. And thus she learned all
my poems by heart. In return, she says, *Dave, you have soft skin
and you're beautiful.* I don't know what to say besides I love you.
I try to speak but I find my mouth is full of bees. My lips part
and the only thing to fly out is bees. My breath is bees. My lungs
are bees. My throat, a black tornado of bees. Suddenly I am
beautiful, and my veins are full of bees. She says, *Why aren't you
talking? Are you in there?* I say, *I'm trying to think of the right words.*

I pull her body close but the hair on my arms is barbed. She says,
Why do you always need the right words? I say, *Bees.* She says,
   I'm leaving,
I say, *Wait.*
Did you know that a bee's sweetest honey is just its vomit?

and she's gone.

    *

I never said love, but I could tell you how she takes her tea.
I could tell you where the honey is.

After Zuko

Yes, I too have known fire. And yes,
I too have wondered if I come from
a burnt people. A people who have always
been ablaze. I have hated my own hands.

I have been prince to a kingdom of folk
and dishonored them. I have worn a white mask.
I have cut my hair to look less like me. I too
have sought to be anything other than the ashes

of another man's sin. I have tried to earn my existence
in a nation that would not claim me. I have scorched
the ones who care most. I have searched the countryside
to find something I always had. And yes,

I have been unworthy of my mother's love.
I have known the right thing to do and done
otherwise. I too have been an exile and a product
of my tribe. Yes, I am still running.

I too am afraid of being a good man. I too
have been beaten by water. Nearly drowned. Emerged.
And still, I would burn a forest down
just to feel the warmth against my skin.

Telepathy at the music festival in Minneapolis

I understand my powers/whenever I am surrounded/there
is only one other Black face in the audience/and we all paid
the same entry price/the white man trippin/on acid wants
to lose his hand/in my afro/only one other person sees this/
the telepathy begins in our pupils/a whole continent of
conversation/with a slight turn of the neck and a focus of
the eyes/she says/*I hate when these people try to touch my
hair*/I reply/*I know right*/by which I mean we have always
been outnumbered/why else would we communicate with
the silence of a stare/in a room that cannot hear me/I learn
the language of a closed mouth/how to look someone in the
eye and know nothing/and everything/we laugh/she says/
white people can't dance/we laugh/the easy joke/is silent/*I know
right*/by this I mean I have always feared a death at hands
that cannot follow a heartbeat/surely this power must be in
our genes/this heritable tremor/this atrophy of a fist/this
audacity of breath/we laugh/we are surrounded/I don't
know if this place was meant for me/I think I can survive/in
the shade

Nest

Between classes, I am often caught looking up
at the family of crows nesting in the corner
of the theater building. In the space between the spikes
designed to keep them away. I notice the shit
before the birds. They rest high and unleash
their waste below. I admire them for what they do
with spit and sticks and loose fabric. Ragtag house.
I suppose you can raise a child anywhere. I worry what will
happen when the youngest chick stretches its wings
into the sharp metal. I can only imagine blood. Still, they are
alive and I am down here scavenging for paper. I am working
for my master's degree. It's impossible to learn a lesson twice.
The feathers pushing their way from my skin. I know
the spikes and choose to stay. I'm being vague. What I mean is
I like these birds because I am sure that they once saw another
bird impale itself on the silver spike and watched the last breath
leak from its breast. And this was a type of schooling.
And still, they nested. Legacy. The joy of choosing where to place
the grave. I'm comfortable
in the sense that I have a bed. Cheddar plate. American progress,
its crows flapping in the winds. Me returning to the task
I enrolled for. Look at the home I've made of paper.

Desdemona

When the race war commences and the shells of bullets
tap dance in the streets, when the generals force us to
 choose sides—I will be your slave. Othello in the sheets

when there are no more streets. Don't call me by my name.
The soldiers will come for necks, spiking severed heads
 on antenna, blonde scalps and afro omens of dangers

to come. My alliance all too clear. I nibble your ear
and croon the name of your house. My lips
 tender to your throat. A bomb detonated south of here

and I go down to give you what we want. In your bed
you call for more. Command me.
 I love being told what my body can do.

I know the difference between hunger and wanting.
I was once America's profit,
 singing spirituals and mapping freedom lines

between stars. Falsettos praising the cool of dawn.
All the while coveting the knowledge of masters. Guns and
 language. They had the guns so I learned to tongue my way

into the royal family. Loyal to my new name. I understood
the truth of captivity once I wed
 my captor. Like the buck licking the barrel, I did

not run. How could the forefathers imagine what I'd do
with their daughters? How could Harriet know
 what would make me come? No, I am not my ancestors'

wildest dreams. I am much too happy here.
Before the war, the marches and boycotts moved us
   into fresher wounds. Each generation promising

   a new comfort to deny. I waited in the water.
Now we've come to burning the dead for heat
   and not trusting the reservoir. Now the flags

   have flown their faces and patience has picked up
a rifle. Now the players take the fight to the playing fields,
   kneeling to the tune of the free. Outside is scorching and here

   I am on top, lashing away. I am tying you to your bedframe
since you like what I do with rope. You say choke me harder
   and I nearly think about it.

In casual conversation, the hood in me
slips out and says

boy look at you. the day you got into college was the first
time your mother cried a tear that didn't hurt. you might've
been too young to remember this but the first time you had
a cheesesteak, you hated it. but I grew on you. I raised you
like all parents raise their children: imperfect and afraid, but
damn if there's not food on the table every night. I watched
your feet hopscotch across this pavement. I was there when
you first learned to say your own name.

there is a difference between leaving home
and deciding not to come back.

college boy I have a question: how long do you pause when
people ask you where you're from? how many answers do
you give? how do you explain the distance between West
Philly and College Street? so many kids die on my blocks so
trust, I understand fear. but I don't got time for forgetting.
for acting like memory ain't a conscious decision.

tell me, do you claim your school before you claim your
home? do you think that will protect you? do you think they
know you like I know you? like I know your blood and veins,
how you didn't know shame until they taught it to you. to
graduate is to pretend to have a dead white man's authority
and maybe that's what this is about. maybe my approval was
not enough so you had to seek it from someone who ain't
want you in the first place.

young bull I buried myself inside you but sometimes the
hood cannot contain itself. sometimes it'll slip up and tell
you to bring that ass here and let me wash your mouth with
soap. you don't need their language to make your breath
valuable. I told you when you was a boy I said

you'd be the one to make it.
now what have you made?

see nowadays, now that you be leavin n shit, I look in the
mirror and think who must I be? am I just something you
had to survive? ain't I more than blackened earth? what's in
a textbook that ain't on my walls? what's in that classroom
that you couldn't find in ya mama's house?

they ask you where you're from and you say West Philly. the
nerve of you, boy who is you to claim me and not look me in
the eye? I don't know you anymore. you sit in that dining
hall eating vegan chicken. out there taking selfies with white
folk, well good for them. I'm glad they have at least one
Black friend. how many of us had to die so you could be their
diversity? there is no such thing as progress. there is only
looking someone in the eye and knowing exactly where they
come from.

but you don't remember the skyline. you don't remember
the sky.

ain't that funny? you used to look up at me and think wow.
what an endless blue.

I could be that forever.

Self-portrait as fuckboy

I can be honest with you. I will kiss anyone who can swipe
me away from myself. An ex told me I'd never know anyone
until I knew how to be alone. I broke up with her & I've been
lonely ever since. So she was wrong. Haha. I'm not alone
though. I could die & I'm sure people would be sad. I spend
lots of time looking in mirrors. I know I am just a pile of
used nests. I am king of feeling my pocket for the headphones
in my ear. I love anyone who can find my phone for me. I can
listen to a song on repeat for 12 hours & still not remember
the lyrics. Did I say "love" earlier? I did. Sorry I meant "am
not looking for." If I needed to, I could close my eyes & put a
name to each of my ex's lips from touch alone. Are you cool
with that? I suppose I am fine with being lips for a few
months. Help. I've fallen & I am quite comfortable in my
bed. You could join me. Not forever but for now. We could
stay here for hours & never have to reply to a text. The rent
man might come take our pillows. He hoards other people's
pillows. It's ok. I can replace the pillows. I have so many
feathers. This is what I offer to you. Bawk. I am a pigeon.
No one sees me when I sleep.

IPhone notes for a powerful poem

Another one about death and god.
God's face is the color of the air so to breathe
is to know God. So yes, there must be a heaven.
Does that make sense?

*

Idea for revenge story: in order to defeat white supremacy,
adopt the voice of a slave on a ship
and sink the whole damn thing. I'd drown too
but everyone loses money or at least gets a little damp

*

Say their names on the way to work.
There. That's something. All the dead are worth something.
They love it when you give them a name. How we become
palatable for brunch or a talk about how complex this is

*

Black skin as a metaphor for darkness/or disappearing at
night/ or missing teeth/or an unlit past/or the ship the sky
and the stars/or everything except the light at the end of the
tunnel/or your father's face and his absence/or just the
absence/or Black skin as a metaphor for

*

Another one died today. Memorize the name and make it a poem.
You're dying too

*

Idea: a remake of *It's a Wonderful Life* and when the angel grants
George Bailey's wish to have never existed, the credits roll

*

Our people have so many ways of knowing death
and still we choose living. God
that's so much pressure

*

Did this English professor really just say he despises hip-hop?
Well, fuck you and your white heaven. Fuck your Gods.
My people
peopled the sky

*

A poem about being sick and tired of being
sick and tired of writing this poem
though I know I haven't risen above it.
I want flowers without the tomb

*

Say my name
so others can speak it too

*

There. A creation. It breathes when I can't. Let anything
I make be my act of God

The barbershop after Prince died

I can think of more Black people who've died young than old.
The grave is the only promise I've ever known to stay true.

Let me die having been worth loving.
Let the need for love be enough.

Let me give what I have. Let me finish what I start.
Let me be young and growing and questioning all
that was handed to me.

Let me have a new song for when the old songs fail.
Let me die when there are no more songs.

The day the sky turned purple, I called home.
There was music playing everywhere.

Turbulence

I can't stop imagining my own death on airplanes. I buckle my seatbelt and a propeller flies through the plane and slices off my arm. I look as my insides stream from the wound. If this doesn't

happen then later the plane will fall slowly and smash into a mountain. I am crushed like a grape inside a fist. My mother asks me to text her every time I board a plane. I never say I love you,

only, "On the flight!" Then my mind begins the dirty work. Visualizing how this could kill me. I read that flying is the safest way to cross distance. Safety requires the accumulation of

knowledge. My mother learned my father was like two different people. His violence snuck up on him, and neither of them saw it coming. In one moment, he'd fill the fridge and the next BAM his

fist would come crashing down. A split pomegranate is how I picture my mother's scalp, before the stitches. Burst open. I shouldn't say that like I was there. I was barely a year. It doesn't

cost my body to imagine. Not really. I know the body is fragile by what I learned was done to my mother's. The price of a lesson: to describe what happened so that it might not happen again.

An SOS in the sand. He lifted her up into the sky and held her there, gasping. There it is again. I don't know what came over me. Sometimes, you make me so angry I just lose control. The pilot loses control and the whole plane rattles. I watch the babies cry. The last time I saw my father was at an airport. Last can have so many meanings. Final. Most recent. Endure. Please stay. I stay

ahead of all the ways I could hurt a person and fly off before they happen. The people I love say I leave and make them feel so far away. I didn't mean to do that. I worry that if I feel too much,

I'll go mad and set the world aflower with something utterly unpredictable. Can you believe that? I am the stranger in the middle seat, bowed by turbulence, gripping wildly in the dark for

your hand. Whispering, will it hurt? I don't want to die. I can see it so clearly. Sometimes this happens. Sometimes the arm lashes out in ways that feel almost instinctive.

Please, don't take me at my word. I always mean to say I'm sorry.

PATRICIDE

Patricide

Like a man, I lied to myself
saying I would do better than my father.
And thus he is lying before me
in a made bed. I crept through darkness
to find him here, asleep in his new life.
Drool warm in his mouth,
nearly at peace. On the wall, there are photos
of a woman I've never met. She's not here.
She doesn't need to be dragged
into this. Nothing looks the way I pictured.

His bed an altar
pressed neatly. Square. Lines for blood
to run. It was no small act
to track him down.
I brought a hammer. Common,
hard, the type used to build
a home.
I won't dwell.
His head is on the pillow and the hammer is in my hands,
raised.

****

Patricide

My mother was terrified that my father
would creep through my childhood window
and drag me into the night. We never knew
when he'd strike. Him, coming back to take
what he thought was his. In other words,
he would come back. I had nightmares of his hands
holding me and not letting go. I locked my doors.
I tucked a screwdriver. I bolted my windows,
but kept watch at night, looking for the man's
eyes through the blinds. In the glass, I'd see a face
looking back at me.

****

Patricide

Once. My mother was not a mother.
Once. My father bends lilies into her hair.
Once. My father decides my name.
Once. My mother loves hard.
Once. My father loves harder.
Once. I laugh on my father's shoulders while he runs.
Once. He runs.
Once rage pulled me far from joy.
Then one became the other.

****

Patricide

Can cruelty be unbelievable?
I can imagine so much. I am told the worst violence
came years before me. A beating I never received.
The scars that aren't on my back. I should be grateful
he wasn't there. And yet, I can't stop seeing.
I dream the color red
and wake to find I've pushed my own tooth clean
through my lower lip.
The tortured voice in my head, whispering.

****

Patricide

Hello.
You had to know it would come to this.
A dead man and his creations.
A living child with work to do.
But give me some credit.
This is all me.
This was a bad plan, I know. Sloppy.
But there is a reason why I am the one who is alive
to tell this story. It would be a comfort to call this generational.
That violence begets violence. My father
as a child, shaking, pissing his pants in front
of his father, who bellowed THE ONLY THING YOU HAVE
TO FEAR IS ME. And his father,
as a teenager, sprinting, gasping for his life,
a white man's dog biting at his heels,
and the man screaming DON'T YOU DARE
LOOK ME IN THE EYES.
That none of these men were ever brought to light
and revenge bled from one hand to the next.
That I had no choice
but to pick up the hammer
and resume the murderous labor.
But where is the fun in that?
Would it kill you to know
that amongst the pearls of sweat and ruby spray
I smiled?

****

Patricide

It wasn't until it was over that I realized
I was the one screaming the whole time.
Even dead, he looks just like me
the way all blood resembles itself.
Now I know what it is like
to hold someone close
as blood, and then see the blood.

I have nothing left to imagine.

My love, what a wonderful home
I've built with you.

****

Patricide

Out of his blood, a ripple. Something new.
First hands then the crown
of a head pushing through the pool. A body
emerges. Then another. Then another.
Crawling from my father's blood
comes a new line of fathers. Men shimmering
scarlet. Scarless and bare. Released
from their blood prison.
They walk past me on their way out,
pat me on the shoulder, whisper
attaboy.

****

Patricide

Now there is me. Alone
in a blood-lit room.
What to do. What to do.

To run like an ancestor, trails of red footprints
in the mud. To leave my mark on everything.
To sit in the mess. So many years it took
for this.

Out of the blood, I lift myself.
Father to one. The night awaiting my arrival.
I look over my shoulder, still holding the hammer.
Who's after me?

NOTES

The title and first line of "TO THE EXTENT X BODY INCLUDING ITS FISTS CONSTITUTE 'WEAPONS'" are taken from a US court document of Officer Darren Wilson's list of admissions.

The epigraph of "Universal experiences" is taken from Indiana University Art Museum. The poem is an ekphrasis on Felrath Hines's "Piano Forte" (1988).

"BARS POETICA: A DISS TRACK" borrows lines from Walt Whitman, 2 Chainz, Archibald MacLeish, and Lil Uzi Vert.

GRATITUDE

To Hanif Abdurraqib for your generous and patient poring through the many versions of this book.

To Sam Cook, Dylan Garity, and everyone else at Button Poetry for supporting these poems since the days of Sweet Tea.

To Ervin A. Johnson for your incredible artwork that made the cover of this book.

To the homies too numerous to name. To every squad and in every iteration. To Alan Zhang, Marcel Logan, Ashley Greaves, Yaa Ampofo, Julia Jenjezwa, Chad Small, Ari Kagan, Nish John, Isy Ibibo, Téa Chai, Eliana Pipes, Gineiris Garcia, and the many more pages I could fill.

To Naomi North for believing I had a book in me before I did.

To Deb Margolin for not letting me stop.

To a few of the many writers whom I have had the gift of knowing and learning from: Alysia Harris, Camille Thomasson Anna Binkovitz, Shanna Alden, Davon Clark, Adriana Ramírez, Will Evans, Claire Schwartz, Marcus Wicker, Xandria Phillips, Anya Richkind.

To my Callaloo cohort, forever searching for the volta: Nicole Homer, Crystal Valentine, Marvin Hodges, Nicholas Nichols, Kassidi Jones, Noor Ibn Najam, Jay Ward, and Portia Bartley.

To the spaces that have showed me community: Greg Pardlo & Vievee Francis at Callaloo. Cornelius Eady, Toi Dericotte, Evie Shockley, Chris Abani, and Robin Coste Lewis at Cave Canem. To SPACE at Ryder Farm. To everyone at the MFA program at UC San Diego.

To my cohort at UCSD: Mara Nelson-Greenberg, Ali Viterbi, Steph Del Rosso, Ava Geyer, Vivian Barnes, Lily Padilla, and Anna Moench.

To WORD at Yale. My first writing home. The oldest and hypest.

To Alex Nguyen, Abigail Carney, Olivia Klevorn, Sophie Dillon, Hayun Cho, Connor Szostak, Rianna Johnson-Levy, Joey Lew, J.T. Flowers, Yuni Chang, Grace Alofe, Alex Zhang, Luna Beller Tadiar, Ashia Ajani, Anita Norman, Fernado Rojas.

To my families. Grandmothers, uncles, cousins, friends, teachers.

To my sister, LaShan.
To my mother, Dawn.
Always.
To love and all of its complications.

I am so happy to be here.

To you, reader. I am glad we found our way to each other.

ACKNOWLEDGMENTS

I am grateful for the editors of the following publications, where versions of these poems appeared:

"I haven't killed my father yet" in *Winter Tangerine*.

"Myths for growing up", "Universal experiences", and "Self-portrait as fuckboy" in *Black Napkin Press*.

"Shark Week" and "Explaining to my aunt that Jesus was Black" in *Apiary Magazine*.

"And the dog say to the cat" and "It don't crack" in *The Misanthropy*.

"TO THE EXTENT . . ." in *BOAAT Press*.

"For Piccolo" and "For Zuko" in *Freeze Ray Poetry*.

"My Train" in *Rattle Magazine*.

"Turbulence" as the winner of the 2018 Rattle Poetry Prize.

"When I say I'm afraid of going bald what I mean is" and "My mother tells me my father was a gorilla" in *Up The Staircase Quarterly*.

"Preparing a meal" in *Pittsburgh Poetry Review*.

"My father's hands" in *Muzzle Magazine*.

ABOUT THE AUTHOR

Dave Harris is a poet and playwright from West Philly. He is a Cave Canem Poetry Fellow, a Callaloo Poetry Fellow, a member of The Working Farm at SPACE on Ryder Farm, and a 2018 Venturous Fellow at The Lark. His full-length collection of poetry, *Patricide*, will be published in May 2019 from Button Poetry. Dave received his B.A. from Yale and is a second year MFA playwright at UC San Diego.

OTHER BOOKS BY BUTTON POETRY

If you enjoyed this book, please consider checking out
some of our others, below. Readers like you allow us to keep
broadcasting and publishing. Thank you!

Neil Hilborn, *Our Numbered Days*
Hanif Willis-Abdurraqib, *The Crown Ain't Worth Much*
Olivia Gatwood, *New American Best Friend*
Donte Collins, *Autopsy*
Melissa Lozada-Oliva, *peluda*
Sabrina Benaim, *Depression & Other Magic Tricks*
William Evans, *Still Can't Do My Daughter's Hair*
Rudy Francisco, *Helium*
Guante, *A Love Song, A Death Rattle, A Battle Cry*
Rachel Wiley, *Nothing Is Okay*
Neil Hilborn, *The Future*
Phil Kaye, *Date & Time*
Andrea Gibson, *Lord of the Butterflies*
Blythe Baird, *If My Body Could Speak*
Desireé Dallagiacomo, *SINK*

Available at buttonpoetry.com/shop and more!